T0381413

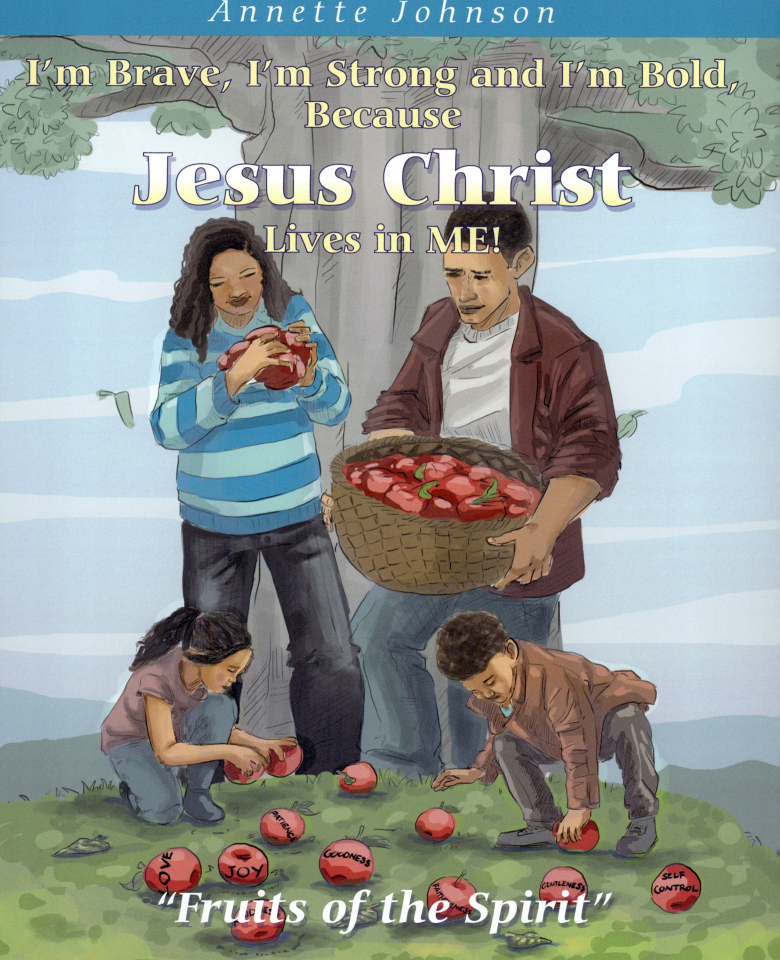

BIBLE CITATION

Scripture quotations marked KJV are from the Holy
Bible, King James Version (Authorized Version).
First published in 1611. Quoted from the KJV Classic
Reference Bible, Copyright © 1983 by The Zondervan
Corporation

Print information available on the last page

Rev. date: 01/02/2019

To order additional copies of this book, contact:
Xlibris
1-888-795-4274
www.Xlibris.com
Orders@Xlibris.com

I'm Brave, I'm Strong and I'm Bold, Because

Jesus Christ

Lives in ME!

"Fruits of the Spirit"

Annette Johnson

INTRODUCTION

READ THE WORDS OUT LOUD

I'm Brave, I'm Strong, and I'm Bold Because "Jesus Christ lives in ME"!

(your name).

"Fruits of the Spirit"

Scripture: Galatians 5:22-23 But the fruit of the Spirit is love, joy, peace, patience, kindness, goodness, faithfulness, gentleness, and self-control.

The Fruits of the Spirit talks about showing and setting the example in demonstrating positive fruit in your attitude, in your heart and in your life.

Let's start reading about the "Fruits of the Spirit":

LOVE (SHOUT LOVE!) Love is unconditional, Jesus is Love. His Love is unconditional Love – meaning (AGAPE) the God kind of Love. Jesus Loves you just the way you are. No matter who you are, no matter where you are from, no matter how young or how old you are and what you have done in life - Jesus Loves you regardless. Always show love to your family, tell your family members everyday "I Love You".

Scripture: 1 Corinthians 13:4-7 Love is patient and kind; love does not envy or boast; it is not arrogant or rude. It does not insist on its own way; it is not irritable or resentful; it does not rejoice at wrongdoing, but rejoices with the truth. Love bears all things, believes all things, hopes all things, and endures all things. God's Love Never Fail.

JOY (SHOUT JOY!) Joy is what you demonstrate in your heart regardless how you feel. If you feel sad or mad, you can always choose joy. To change that feeling into joy, start laughing, start smiling, and start thinking positive thoughts in your mind – your feeling will change from sad or mad to joy. So, choose joy today and change your attitude before you go to school, before you go to church or sitting at the dinner table to talk with your family. Always choose to have an attitude of joy.

Scripture: Isaiah 55:12 "For you shall go out in joy and be led forth in peace; the mountains and the hills before you shall break forth into singing, and all the trees of the field shall clap their hands.

PEACE (SHOUT PEACE!) Peace is thinking positive thoughts and mediating on good things in life. For example, have you ever sat at your window and watch the rain showers or watch snow falling to the ground or watch beautiful sunsets or watch a full moon coming up before it's dark outside or watch colorful leaves falling from trees during the fall months, or watch clouds moving in the skies – all examples of peaceful scenes. Your heavenly Father loves you so much He created beautiful things for you to enjoys and see. If you have not, take some time one day and sit on your porch or look out the window after school or chose one Saturday evening sitting in a quiet place and watch God's creation. Make sure you turn off the TV, radio and no video games.

Scripture: Isaiah 26:3 You keep him in perfect peace whose mind is stayed on you, because he trusts in you.

PATIENCE (SHOUT PATIENCE!) Patience is another area in life where you have to learn to take turns, learning to share with a good attitude, learning to wait your turn, waiting on answers when asked a question, being patience to save your money and not quick to send it all. While waiting, you have to learn not to get discouraged, but keep a good attitude by staying positive, encouraged and being motivated about everything in life. Strive always to have a positive attitude about everything – learn to be patience and wait.

Scripture: James 5:7 Be patient, therefore, brothers, until the coming of the Lord. See how the farmer waits for the precious fruit of the earth, being patient about it, until it receives the early and the late rains.

KINDNESS (SHOUT KINDNESS!) Kindness is a word that's let you know to show respect to your elders such as your dad, your mom, granddad, grandma, uncles, aunts, all who are in authority positions. Kindness is being nice to your friends at church, at school and neighbors. Learn to show kindness in your heart towards people.

Scripture: Colossians 3:12-13 Put on then, as God's chosen ones, holy and beloved, compassionate hearts, kindness, humility, meekness, and patience, bearing with one another and, if one has a complaint against another, forgiving each other; as the Lord has forgiven you, so you also must forgive.

GOODNESS (SHOUT GOODNESS!) Goodness is demonstrated from your heart – showing goodness is having a heart to give someone who has a need. Such as giving unwanted clothes to the homeless shelter, giving to your local church, serving food, making boxes of goodies for the military members or providing Christmas gifts for children who are less fortune then you. Being a blessing to someone is an awesome opportunity, praying for someone, being a good listener and doing a good deed in your community.

Scripture: Acts 10:38 How God anointed Jesus of Nazareth with the Holy Spirit and with power. He went about doing good and healing all who were oppressed by the devil, for God was with him.

FAITHFULNESS (SHOUT FAITHFULNESS!) Faithfulness is believing by faith as you pray – your heavenly Father in Jesus name hears and answers according to the bible (His word). He said in His word (the bible) to ask that your joy may be full. Do you like to receive answers to your prayer when you ask Him? Yes. Our Heavenly Father Loves when we pray to Him in Jesus name. That means you trust Him to hear and answer your prayers.

Scripture: Ephesians 6:18 Praying always without ceasing and Psalm 55:17 Evening, and morning, and at noon, will I pray, and cry aloud and He will shall hear my voice.

GENTLENESS: **(SHOUT GENTLENESS!)** Gentleness is a fruit that is on the inside of you also, in your heart and gentleness will show in your actions. People will see the fruit in you, your attitude. A humble and gentle person will demonstrate how he or she acts with animals, how you handle or use other people things, especially handling or taking care of someone personal items. You are to be mindful not to destroy or damage other people things.

Scripture: Titus 3:2 To speak evil of no one, to avoid quarreling, to be gentle, and to show perfect courtesy toward all people.

SELF-CONTROL (SHOUT SELF-CONTROL!) Self-Control – Do you need help with self-control? There's a scripture in the bible John 14:26 states the Holy Spirit is your comforter, helper, strengthener, and standby who will teach you all things and remind you of all things. When you received Jesus Christ in your heart, the Holy Spirit comes to live in our heart at the same time (He's our unseen partner).

The Holy Spirit is our helper to help us and remind us to maintain self-control. He will help you to make the right decision in life – just ask Him and listen for the answer. Example: Okay, Holy Spirit help me not to lie, Holy Spirit help me to eat the right foods, Holy Spirit help me to choose to love verse hate, Holy Spirit help me to think good thoughts in my mind and not to have negative thoughts, Holy Spirit help me in all areas in my life (going to church and to read my bible, going to school, or at home - everywhere).

Scripture: 2 Timothy 1:7 For God did not give us a spirit of timidity (of cowardice, of craven and cringing and fawning fear), but He has given us a spirit of power, and of love, of a calm and well-balanced mind, discipline and self-control.

Confession of Faith (speak out loud daily) say:

Today I will think, I will talk, and I will speak the "Fruits of the Spirit"

- I will **love** people and I will **love** myself

- I will choose to have an attitude of **joy** everyday

- I will have **peace** in my mind thinking positive thoughts

- I will learn to wait and have an good attitude of **patience** towards people and myself

- I will be **kind** and **good** in my heart in life

- I will have **faith** in God, walking by faith and not by sight

- I will be **gentle** in life

- I will maintain **self-control** at all times

Confession of Faith:

I will believe in Jesus by faith, I will stand, I will apply the word of God, I will speak and I will demonstrate in my life the "Fruits of the Spirit" every day and I will ask the Holy Spirit to help me in Jesus name.

Prayer of Salvation

Jesus come live in my heart, change me and transform me to imitate YOU. Use me, help me, teach me – So Holy Spirit led, guide and direct me daily in Jesus name. Holy Spirit help me to understand when I read the bible to receive wisdom, knowledge and insight.

Jesus You are my Superhero and YOU live in ME!

(_____)

YOUR NAME

Annette Johnson words: I thank my Heavenly Father for the opportunity to write this book for children. Children need to know how much God loves them and He has a plan for their lives. Parents need to read and speak God's words over our children lives letting them know they are unique individuals on the earth. It's time for our children to know to speak positive words, to be brave, to be strong, to be bold in Jesus name. In Ephesians 5:1 states "Therefore be imitators of God (copy Him and follow His example), as well-beloved children (imitate their father). We need to intimate our heavenly Father so let's get start now while they are in the womb. In 2 Corinthians 6:18 AMP our children need to know who they are – sons and daughters of God. Parent it our duty to teach them biblical principles, to grow up to be strong men and women of God, they're the next generation.

Printed in the United States
By Bookmasters